www.providencebooks.net

Publisher Contact

Email:contact@providencebooks.net

Social media: facebook.com/providencebooks

Acknowledgements

The team at Providence Books would like to thank our friends, family, suppliers and customers for making our vision of creating the highest-quality books a reality. Thanks for purchasing and enjoy the quotes!

This page is intentionally left blank

This page is intentionally left blank

A family is very special. So when a family splits up, it's not good, it's never good.

Aung San Suu Kyi

A more significant phase should mean serious political dialogue.

Aung San Suu Kyi

A revolution simply means great change, significant change, and that's how I'm defining it - great change for the better, brought about through non-violent means.

Aung San Suu Kyi

After all it was my father who founded the Burmese army and I do have a sense of warmth towards the Burmese army.

Aung San Suu Kyi

All military regimes use security as the reason why they should remain in power. It's nothing original.

Aung San Suu Kyi

All repressive laws must be revoked, and laws introduced to protect the rights of the people.

Aung San Suu Kyi

As long as there is no law in Burma, any individual here can be arrested at any time.

Aung San Suu Kyi

Assuming the chairmanship of ASEAN isn't going to do anything about improving the lives of people.

Aung San Suu Kyi

At this age, I should be leading a quiet life.

Aung San Suu Kyi

Books always help.

Aung San Suu Kyi

Burmese authors and artists can play the role that artists everywhere play. They help to mold the outlook of a society - not the whole outlook, and they are not the only ones to mold the outlook of society, but they have an important role to play there.

Aung San Suu Kyi

By helping others, you will learn how to help yourselves.

Aung San Suu Kyi

Confidence-building is not something that can go on forever. If it goes on forever then it becomes counterproductive.

Aung San Suu Kyi

Democracy is when the people keep a government in check.

Aung San Suu Kyi

Dissidents can't be dissidents forever; we are dissidents because we don't want to be dissidents.

Aung San Suu Kyi

Even one voice can be heard loudly all over the world in this day and age.

Aung San Suu Kyi

Every government must consider the security of the country. That is just part of the responsibilities of any government. But true security can only come out of unity within a country where there are so many ethnic nationalities.

Aung San Suu Kyi

Fires of suffering and strife are raging around the world.

Aung San Suu Kyi

For me, 'revolution' simply means radical change.

Aung San Suu Kyi

Frankly, if you do politics, you should not be thinking about your dignity.

Aung San Suu Kyi

Freedom and democracy are dreams you never give up.

Aung San Suu Kyi

Fundamental violations of human rights always lead to people feeling less and less human.

Aung San Suu Kyi

History is always changing.

Aung San Suu Kyi

Human beings the world over need freedom and security that they may be able to realize their full potential.

Aung San Suu Kyi

Human beings want to be free and however long they may agree to stay locked up, to stay oppressed, there will come a time when they say 'That's it.' Suddenly they find themselves doing something that they never would have thought they would be doing, simply because of the human instinct that makes them turn their face towards freedom.

Aung San Suu Kyi

Humor is one of the best ingredients of survival.

Aung San Suu Kyi

I am not unaware of the saying that more tears have been shed over wishes granted than wishes denied.

Aung San Suu Kyi

I am prepared to talk with anyone. I have no personal grudge toward anybody.

Aung San Suu Kyi

I could listen to the radio and I had access to books from time to time. Not all the time.

Aung San Suu Kyi

I do not hold to non-violence for moral reasons, but for political and practical reasons.

Aung San Suu Kyi

I do protect human rights, and I hope I shall always be looked up as a champion of human rights.

Aung San Suu Kyi

I don't believe in professional dissidents. I think it's just a phase, like adolescence.

Aung San Suu Kyi

I don't think I have achieved anything that I can really be proud of.

Aung San Suu Kyi

I don't think of myself as unbreakable. Perhaps I'm just rather flexible and adaptable.

Aung San Suu Kyi

I don't think you can work on feelings in politics, apart from anything else, political change can come very unexpectedly, sometimes overnight when you least expect it.

Aung San Suu Kyi

I don't understand why people say that I am full of courage. I feel terribly nervous.

Aung San Suu Kyi

I don't want Burma to be a basket case forever.

Aung San Suu Kyi

I don't want to be president, but I want to be free to decide whether or not I want to be president of this country.

Aung San Suu Kyi

I don't want to see the military falling. I want to see the military rising to dignified heights of professionalism and true patriotism.

Aung San Suu Kyi

I feel that the BBC World Service is not as versatile as it used to be - or perhaps I'm not listening at the right times.

Aung San Suu Kyi

I felt that it was my duty not to senselessly waste my time. And since I didn't want to waste my time, I tried to accomplish as much as possible.

Aung San Suu Kyi

I have been free for more than a month. Some people may think that that is long enough. Others may think that that is not quite long enough.

Aung San Suu Kyi

I haven't heard any music on the BBC World Service in a long time. Maybe I'm listening at the wrong times. But not one single piece of music.

Aung San Suu Kyi

I knew some of the army quite well.

Aung San Suu Kyi

I learned to work on a computer years before I was placed under house arrest. Fortunately I had two laptops when I was under house arrest - one an Apple and one a different operating system. I was very proud of that because I know how to use both systems.

Aung San Suu Kyi

I look forward to trying the Internet.

Aung San Suu Kyi

I only used a cell phone for the first time after I was released. I had difficulty coping with it because it seemed so small and insubstantial.

Aung San Suu Kyi

I saw many aspects of the country which I needed to see in order that I might know what we need to do.

Aung San Suu Kyi

I think I should be active politically. Because I look upon myself as a politician. That's not a dirty work you know. Some people think that there are something wrong with politicians. Of course, something wrong with some politicians.

Aung San Suu Kyi

I think I was the healthiest prisoner of conscience in the world.

Aung San Suu Kyi

I think by now I have made it fairly clear that I am not very happy with the word hope. I don't believe in people just hoping.

Aung San Suu Kyi

I think sometimes if you are alone, you are freer because your time is your own.

Aung San Suu Kyi

I think when the people in Burma stop thinking about whether or not they're free, it'll mean that they're free.

Aung San Suu Kyi

I think, if you have enough inner resources, then you can live in isolation for long periods of time and not feel diminished by it.

Aung San Suu Kyi

I was a bit of a coward when I was small. I was terribly frightened of the dark.

Aung San Suu Kyi

I was heartened that people everywhere want certain basic freedoms, even if they live in a totally different cultural environment.

Aung San Suu Kyi

I was surprised by the response of young people because there is a perception that those younger than the 1988 generation are not interested in politics.

Aung San Suu Kyi

I wish people wouldn't think of me as a saint - unless they agree with the definition of a saint that a saint's a sinner who goes on trying.

Aung San Suu Kyi

I would like to have seen my sons growing up.

Aung San Suu Kyi

I'm feeling a little delicate.

Aung San Suu Kyi

I'm not the only one working for democracy in Burma - there are so many people who have worked for it because they believe that this is the only way we can maintain the dignity of our people.

Aung San Suu Kyi

I'm rather inclined to liking people.

Aung San Suu Kyi

I've always been strongly on the side of non-violence.

Aung San Suu Kyi

I've always said that the more coordinated the efforts of the international community are, the better it will be for democracy in Burma.

Aung San Suu Kyi

I've always tried to explain democracy is not perfect. But it gives you a chance to shape your own destiny.

Aung San Suu Kyi

I've been repeating ad nauseam that we in Burma, we are weak with regard to the culture of negotiated compromises, that we have to develop the ability to achieve such compromises.

Aung San Suu Kyi

If I advocate cautious optimism it is not because I do not have faith in the future but because I do not want to encourage blind faith.

Aung San Suu Kyi

If I was afraid of being killed, I would never speak out against the government.

Aung San Suu Kyi

If I were the blushing kind, I would blush to be called a hero.

Aung San Suu Kyi

If you can make people understand why freedom is so important through the arts, that would be a big help.

Aung San Suu Kyi

If you choose to do something, then you shouldn't say it's a sacrifice, because nobody forced you to do it.

Aung San Suu Kyi

If you look at the democratic process as a game of chess, there have to be many, many moves before you get to checkmate. And simply because you do not make any checkmate in three moves does not mean it's stalemate. There's a vast difference between no checkmate and stalemate. This is what the democratic process is like.

Aung San Suu Kyi

If you want to bring an end to long-standing conflict, you have to be prepared to compromise.

Aung San Suu Kyi

In general people feel more relaxed about participating in politics. They aren't frightened as they used to be.

Aung San Suu Kyi

In politics, you also have to be cautiously optimistic.

Aung San Suu Kyi

In terms of the history of a far reaching movement, 20 years is not that long.

Aung San Suu Kyi

In the end, I think people prefer the good to win rather than the bad.

Aung San Suu Kyi

It could achieve a lot if everyone in Burma could stop saying something is good if it is not good, or say something is just if it is not just.

Aung San Suu Kyi

It doesn't seem right for anybody to get so much attention.

Aung San Suu Kyi

It is not power that corrupts but fear. Fear of losing power corrupts those who wield it and fear of the scourge of power corrupts those who are subject to it.

Aung San Suu Kyi

It is often in the name of cultural integrity as well as social stability and national security that democratic reforms based on human rights are resisted by authoritarian governments.

Aung San Suu Kyi

Maybe it is something to do with age, but I have become fonder of poetry than of prose.

Aung San Suu Kyi

More people, especially young people, are realising that if they want change, they've got to go about it themselves - they can't depend on a particular person, i.e. me, to do all the work. They are less easy to fool than they used to be, they now know what's going on all over the world.

Aung San Suu Kyi

My attitude is, do as much as I can while I'm free. And if I'm arrested I'll still do as much as I can.

Aung San Suu Kyi

My attitude to peace is rather based on the Burmese definition of peace - it really means removing all the negative factors that destroy peace in this world. So peace does not mean just putting an end to violence or to war, but to all other factors that threaten peace, such as discrimination, such as inequality, poverty.

Aung San Suu Kyi

My opinion is the greatest reward that any government could get is the approval of the people. If the people are happy and the people are at peace and the government has done something for them, that's the greatest reward I think any government could hope for.

Aung San Suu Kyi

No, I was never afraid.

Aung San Suu Kyi

Of course I regret not having been able to spend time with my family.

Aung San Suu Kyi

Once serious political dialogue has begun, the international community can assume that we have achieved genuine progress along the road to real democratisation.

Aung San Suu Kyi

One person alone can't do anything as important as bringing genuine democracy to a country.

Aung San Suu Kyi

One should mature over 20 years.

Aung San Suu Kyi

One wants to be together with one's family. That's what families are about.

Aung San Suu Kyi

Peace as a goal is an ideal which will not be contested by any government or nation, not even the most belligerent.

Aung San Suu Kyi

People keep saying I've changed. I used to be confrontational. But I'm - I haven't changed. It was - it's just that circumstances have changed.

Aung San Suu Kyi

People must work in unison.

Aung San Suu Kyi

Regime is made up of people, so I do put faces to regimes and governments, so I feel that all human beings have the right to be given the benefit of the doubt, and they also have to be given the right to try to redeem themselves if they so wish.

Aung San Suu Kyi

Sanctions and boycotts would be tied to serious political dialogue.

Aung San Suu Kyi

Sanctions are not really an economic weapon.

Aung San Suu Kyi

Since we live in this world, we have to do our best for this world.

Aung San Suu Kyi

Sometimes I think that a parody of democracy could be more dangerous than a blatant dictatorship, because that gives people an opportunity to avoid doing anything about it.

Aung San Suu Kyi

Suffering degrades, embitters and enrages.

Aung San Suu Kyi

The Nobel Peace Prize opened up a door in my heart.

Aung San Suu Kyi

The best way to help Burma is to empower the people of Burma, to help us have enough self-confidence to obtain what we want for ourselves.

Aung San Suu Kyi

The democracy process provides for political and social change without violence.

Aung San Suu Kyi

The history of the world shows that peoples and societies do not have to pass through a fixed series of stages in the course of development.

Aung San Suu Kyi

The judiciary in Burma is not independent. It's widely known, everybody knows that.

Aung San Suu Kyi

The judiciary must be strengthened and released from political interference.

Aung San Suu Kyi

The people have given me their support; they have given me their trust and confidence. My colleagues have suffered a lot in order to give me support. I do not look upon my life as a sacrifice at all.

Aung San Suu Kyi

The struggle for democracy and human rights in Burma is a struggle for life and dignity. It is a struggle that encompasses our political, social and economic aspirations.

Aung San Suu Kyi

The value systems of those with access to power and of those far removed from such access cannot be the same. The viewpoint of the privileged is unlike that of the underprivileged.

Aung San Suu Kyi

There is a time to be quiet and a time to talk.

Aung San Suu Kyi

There is so much that we need to do for our country. I don't think that we can afford to wait.

Aung San Suu Kyi

This was the way I was brought up to think of politics, that politics was to do with ethics, it was to do with responsibility, it was to do with service, so I think I was conditioned to think like that, and I'm too old to change now.

Aung San Suu Kyi

To be forgotten, is to die a little.

Aung San Suu Kyi

War is not the only arena where peace is done to death.

Aung San Suu Kyi

We always think that everybody can do a little bit more, if not a lot more.

Aung San Suu Kyi

We are not out to boast that there is so much percentage of growth per year. Our real concern is how it affects the lives of people, the future of our country.

Aung San Suu Kyi

We want to empower our people; we want to strengthen them; we want to provide them with the kind of qualifications that will enable them to build up their own country themselves.

Aung San Suu Kyi

We will not change in matters of policy until such time as dialogue has begun.

Aung San Suu Kyi

What I have experienced is nothing compared to what political prisoners in prisons suffer.

Aung San Suu Kyi

What does Burma have to give the United States? We can give you the opportunity to engage with people who are ready and willing to change a society.

Aung San Suu Kyi

Whatever help we may want from the international community now or in the future, we want to make sure that this help is tailored to help our people to help themselves.

Aung San Suu Kyi

When I was under house arrest, it was the BBC that spoke to me - I listened.

Aung San Suu Kyi

When the Nobel Committee chose to honor me, the road I had chosen of my own free will became a less lonely path to follow.

Aung San Suu Kyi

When we think of the state of the economy, we are not thinking in terms of money flow. We are thinking in terms of the effect on everyday lives of people.

Aung San Suu Kyi

When you decide to follow a certain path, you should follow it to the end and not be diverted from it for personal reasons.

Aung San Suu Kyi

With the right kind of institutions, starting with the rule of law, Burma could progress very quickly.

Aung San Suu Kyi

You cannot compromise unless people talk to you.

Aung San Suu Kyi

This page is intentionally left blank

This page is intentionally left blank

This page is intentionally left blank

This page is intentionally left blank

This page is intentionally left blank

www.ingramcontent.com/pod-product-compliance
Lightning Source LLC
Chambersburg PA
CBHW061939280526
45787CB00004B/1656